Essential Issues

MENTAL

DISORDERS

Essential Issues

MENTAL
DISORDERS

BY COURTNEY FARRELL

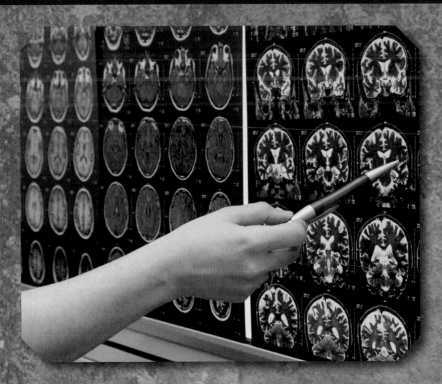

Content Consultant
Sondra E. Solomon, PhD
University of Vermont, Department of Psychology

ABDO
Publishing Company

CREDITS

Published by ABDO Publishing Company, 8000 West 78th Street,
Edina, Minnesota 55439. Copyright © 2010 by Abdo Consulting
Group, Inc. International copyrights reserved in all countries. No
part of this book may be reproduced in any form without written
permission from the publisher. The Essential Library™ is a
trademark and logo of ABDO Publishing Company.

Printed in the United States of America,
North Mankato, Minnesota
102009
012010

 PRINTED ON RECYCLED PAPER

Editor: Holly Saari
Copy Editor: Rebecca Rowell
Interior Design and Production: Becky Daum
Cover Design: Becky Daum

Library of Congress Cataloging-in-Publication Data
Farrell, Courtney.
  Mental disorders / Courtney Farrell.
    p. cm. — (Essential issues)
  Includes bibliographical references and index.
  ISBN 978-1-60453-956-1
  1. Mental illness—Juvenile literature. 2. Mental illness—Social
aspects—Juvenile literature. I. Title.
  RC460.2.F37 2010
  362.196'89—dc22

                    2009029942

TABLE OF CONTENTS

Brooke Shields wrote about her experience in her 2005 book,
Down Came the Rain: My Journey Through Postpartum Depression.

INDIVIDUAL AND
SOCIETAL RIGHTS

In May 2005, Brooke Shields found herself in the national spotlight. As a famous model and actress, Shields was used to being in such a position. This time, however, the circumstances of her fame were far different.

Shields had become the center of a national debate about mental disorders.

A new mother, Shields had recently recovered from postpartum depression. This mental disorder affects some new mothers with symptoms of continued sadness, unreasonable feelings of worthlessness and guilt, and thoughts of harming themselves or their babies. At her lowest points, Shields thought about suicide. She wished her baby would disappear. To recover from this episode, Shields relied on antidepressants as well as psychiatric counseling. Eventually, she tapered off her medicines and made a full recovery.

Shields detailed her experience in her book *Down Came the Rain: My Journey Through Postpartum Depression*, which was published in May 2005. Her story unexpectedly became a topic of conversation for actor Tom

Postpartum Depression

According to the respected Mayo Clinic, many new mothers experience some sadness after childbirth. Referred to as "baby blues," symptoms generally last from a few days to a few weeks and may include mood swings, anxiety, sadness, irritability, crying, decreased concentration, and trouble sleeping. In addition, 10 percent of new mothers are estimated to experience postpartum depression, which has stronger, longer-lasting symptoms that may include loss of appetite, insomnia, intense irritability, overwhelming fatigue, lack of joy, feelings of guilt, severe mood swings, difficulty bonding with the baby, withdrawal from loved ones, and thoughts of harming oneself or the baby.

Cruise. A Scientologist, Cruise thinks psychiatry is a pseudoscience. On the *Today Show*, Cruise faulted Shields for treating her condition with medication. He said:

> But what happens, the antidepressant, all it does is mask the problem. There's ways, [with] vitamins and through exercise and various things. . . . I'm not saying that [the mental disorder] isn't real. That's not what I'm saying. That's an alteration of what I'm saying. I'm saying that drugs aren't the answer.[1]

On July 1, Shields responded to Cruise's remarks in a guest column for the *New York Times*. She criticized Cruise's view. At the same time, she welcomed the opportunity his remarks had created. They allowed her to address the misconceptions and to make known the wide prevalence of the illness. She wrote:

> Since writing about my experiences with the disease, I have been approached by many women who have told me their stories and thanked me for opening up about a topic that is often not discussed because of fear, shame or lack of support and information.[2]

Shields acknowledged that she would not be the parent she had become without having received the help she needed. She also advocated for a

Actor Tom Cruise publicly denounced how Brooke Shields treated her postpartum depression.

larger awareness and understanding of postpartum depression, and she urged other new mothers who experienced depression symptoms to get help.

Shields's experience is not uncommon. Mental disorders are more common than many might imagine. And having a mental disorder makes one vulnerable to criticism—in a way that physical illnesses do not. Shields is one in a long line of people with mental disorders who have been misunderstood, stigmatized, and discriminated against.

What Is a Mental Disorder?

In 2000, the *Diagnostic and Statistical Manual of Mental Disorders (DSM-IV-TR)* defined a mental disorder as:

> *[a] clinically significant behavioral or psychological syndrome or pattern that occurs in an individual and that is associated with present distress . . . or disability . . . or with a significantly increased risk of suffering, death, pain, disability, or an important loss of freedom.* [3]

Mental disorders range in severity. They can cause minor problems or be completely debilitating. Some mental disorders are depression, schizophrenia, and bipolar disorder. Symptoms of mental disorders are not considered part of a person's normal response to a life event. For example, sadness and grief over the loss of a loved one do not automatically indicate a mental disorder. Also, deviating from what society considers normal does not mean a person has a mental disorder.

Until 1973, homosexuality was considered a mental disorder, but that is no longer the case.

According to the National Institute of Mental Health, approximately 26 percent of U.S. citizens ages 18 and older experience a diagnosable mental disorder each year. Based on the 2004 census population, that number is more than 57 million people per year.

Key Issues

People with mental disorders were once denied the most basic human rights and

---

Diagnosing Mental Disorders

The American Psychiatric Association publishes the *Diagnostic and Statistical Manual of Mental Disorders (DSM-IV-TR)*. The *DSM-IV-TR* lists a variety of mental disorders and their specific clinical signs to assist health care professionals when diagnosing their patients. Providing a diagnosis helps the treatment of patients by the health care industry as well as by insurers. Common signs and symptoms of a mental disorder include the following emotions and behaviors:

- Unending sadness: Grieving over the loss of a relationship or loved one is normal, but if the grief never ends, the sufferer needs help.
- Losing control: Delusions, hallucinations, out-of-control emotions, and feelings of invincibility are likely signs of a mental disorder.
- Reckless behavior: In some individuals, reckless behavior can signal a mental disorder.
- Hurting people, pets, or property: Those who torture animals often progress to targeting people.

While the book is primarily used by health care professionals, the *DSM-IV-TR* may help people determine if they, a friend, or a family member should see a mental health professional for assessment and possible treatment.

National Institute of Mental Health

The National Institute of Mental Health (NIMH) is a government agency. It is part of the National Institutes of Health, which is a facet of the larger U.S. Department of Health and Human Services. According to NIMH, its mission "is to transform the understanding and treatment of mental illnesses through basic and clinical research, paving the way for prevention, recovery and cure."[4]

institutionalized under horrific conditions. Those mistreatments have been corrected, but solutions continue to be complicated and debated.

Several key issues surround the topic. Some mental health professionals believe too many mental disorders go undiagnosed and untreated, while others believe normal human problems are being falsely diagnosed as mental disorders. Additional debates center on how best to treat mental disorders, whether mental disorders are as legitimate as physical disorders, and how people with mental disorders should be treated under the law. Each of these challenging topics addresses the same issue: how society can protect the rights of those with mental disorders while still protecting the best interests of the public.

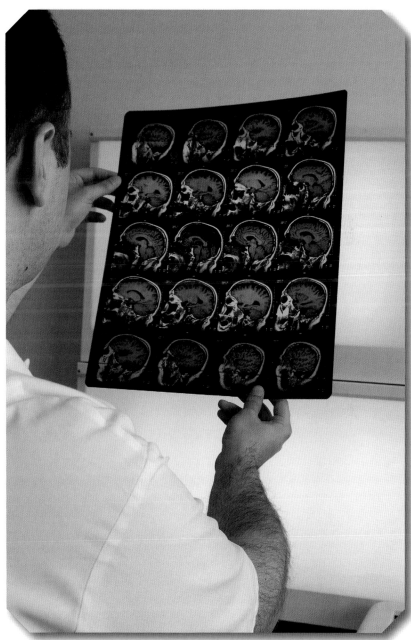

*Medical professionals continue to research and study the brain
to better understand mental disorders.*

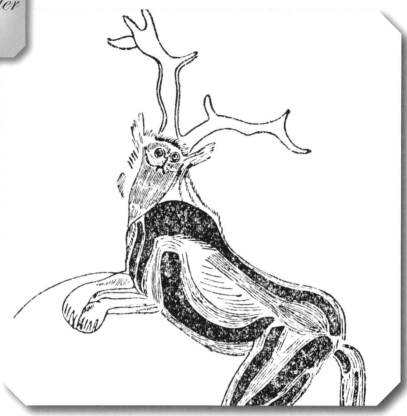

A sketch of The Sorcerer, *a cave painting that likely depicted a supernatural healer who was believed to drive away evil spirits*

A History of Mental Disorders

Mental disorders have likely existed as long as human beings have. Throughout history, attitudes and beliefs about mental disorders—their causes and treatments—have changed.

Ancient civilizations believed that evil spirits or demons caused mental disorders. In Ariège, France, cave paintings dated at 13,000 BCE depict primitive people's belief that mental disorders had supernatural causes. One painting, *The Sorcerer*, shows a creature with human feet and deer antlers. He may have been a god or a healer who could drive "evil spirits" out of the afflicted.

Burials in Ariège reveal that an early form of surgery called trepanation was a treatment for mental disorders. In this procedure, a hole was drilled in the patient's skull and a circle of bone was removed. The brain was exposed but not damaged, and the scalp was stretched back over the hole. Historians suspect that these holes were made to release evil spirits from the brains of people with mental disorders.

Normal and Disordered

Behavior that is considered normal depends on society and changes over time. In 1851, Southern physician Samuel Cartwright identified two so-called mental disorders of slaves. The first, called *Drapetomia*, supposedly caused slaves to run away from their masters. The second, *Dysaethesia Aethiopica*, made slaves lethargic and dull. Neither of these is a real disorder. Escape would now be seen as adaptive and healthy.

EARLY MENTAL HEALTH CARE

In Egypt around 2850 BCE, a medical facility began more sophisticated treatment, including dream analyses and medication. Within the facility's pleasant surroundings, opium calmed agitated patients who were believed to be suffering from magical maladies. Patients wore sacred amulets of protection and invoked the power of the gods to aid them. Patients went boating on the Nile River, and they attended concerts and dances.

Ancient Greeks and Romans generally shared the Egyptian approach, using humane treatment for the mentally ill. Still, the most common belief among Greeks and Romans was that the gods doled out mental disorders, making them out of humans' control. This belief began to change in the fifth and fourth centuries BCE, when reason became more valued as a way of understanding the world, and new ideas about the mind began to take shape.

The Greek physician Hippocrates used medicine to show that diseases had natural rather than supernatural causes. He thought mental disorders came from four fluids in the body: phlegm, blood, yellow bile, and black bile. Differing levels of these fluids in the body led to different ailments.

The medical facility in Egypt that treated people with mental disorders is linked to the temple built by Imhotep.

For example, melancholia and depression were caused by high levels of black bile. These theories were accepted into the late nineteenth century.

MEDIEVAL EUROPE

While Greece and Rome were advocating reason and humane treatment, other parts of Western Europe took a very different approach. Society relied upon religion as an explanation for mental disorders, and people with them were treated poorly.

In the early Middle Ages, families took responsibility for relatives with mental disorders. These "disruptive" family members were kept in small rooms or in crates called lunatic boxes.

By the late Middle Ages, prejudice against people with mental disorders had increased. One reason for this growing intolerance was the dominance of Christianity and the religion's belief that a person's sinful thoughts and deeds caused insanity. Church officials targeted people with mental disorders, accusing them of conspiring with the devil. Harold G. Koenig is a psychiatrist who explained the treatment of people with mental disorders during that time:

> Almost all mentally ill persons [many of them elders living alone] were considered witches or sorcerers,

The Inquisition

The Inquisition was a tribunal of the Catholic Church that punished heretics, people whose beliefs differed from those of religious authorities. Inquisitors visited villages and investigated the accused. Folk healers and the mentally ill were labeled as witches, and then they were tortured and killed. Torture was also used to extract confessions of heresy. Victims were burned at the stake in public spectacles. The Inquisition lasted approximately from the thirteenth century to the nineteenth century in Western Europe.

and hundreds of thousands of people were burned in a cooperative effort of church and state.[1]

As a result, families were likely to keep relatives with mental disorders a secret, often by confining, institutionalizing, or abandoning them.

Punishment was thought to be the only hope for the souls of people with mental disorders. Some people believed physical suffering could drive their demons out. Inadequately trained physicians treated mental patients cruelly.

Asylums

Medieval mental hospitals were frightening prisons where the inhabitants were often isolated in dark chambers. Cell doors and walls did not have windows, just peepholes and a slot in which to push food. Some inmates were locked in cages so small there was room only to lie down: rest was believed to be curative. Others were shackled to walls, unable to even move out of their own excrement. Chambers were cold and damp, and the moldy food rations were scarce.

In many institutions, inmates were tortured. Vesicants, chemicals that burn and blister, were applied to their skin. Foreheads were branded with hot irons to release demonic vapors from the brain. Bloodletting was also believed to be beneficial, but it only weakened already ill patients.

In England, the hospital of St. Mary of Bethlehem was converted to an asylum, a hospital for the mentally ill, in 1402. Bedlam, as it was known, offered tours to citizens who wanted to gawk at the caged inmates. Visitors were chilled by the awful howling of some prisoners and by others begging for help. The artist William Hogarth painted a scene from Bedlam that showed male and female prisoners housed together in a large, chaotic group.

Not all asylum inmates were mentally ill. During the Middle Ages, beggars and disabled people could also be wrongly labeled insane and become institutionalized. Poor people were collected in roundups

A Welcoming Village

In the Middle Ages, the Flemish village of Geel was the site of the shrine to St. Dymphna, patron saint of those suffering from mental disorders. In the fourteenth century, groups of those with mental disorders began to make pilgrimages there, hoping for a cure. Villagers took patients into their homes. The patients were treated kindly, and they helped their hosts as they were able with household and farm chores. Peculiar behavior was gently corrected rather than punished. Geel remained a colony for people with mental disorders into the early twentieth century.

by city authorities looking to clean up the streets. One such roundup took place in sixteenth-century France, when approximately 6,000 people were locked up in Paris's General Hospital.

HUMANITARIAN REFORM

Not everyone during the Middle Ages thought people with mental disorders deserved harsh treatment. Juan Luis Vives, born in 1492, was a Spanish Catholic from a family of Jewish converts. At this time, Church officials of the Spanish Inquisition were persecuting Jews who had converted to Christianity. Inquisitors executed Vives's father and numerous other family members. Vives escaped his country. Later, from the safety of a monastery, he spoke out against the Church's idea that the devil was behind mental disorders. Such outspokenness seems expected in the modern world, but Vives would have been killed for it had the inquisitors caught him.

Mental health care began to take a turn for the better during the rule of King George III in England. In approximately 1765, George started experiencing fits of madness. Periods of insanity would come and go, causing political upheaval. Despite his status, George was placed in a straightjacket and chained to a chair in his palace apartment. The harsh treatment of the king caused a scandal, bringing attention to the suffering of common patients. The British began to institute reforms in mental health care, gradually turning madhouses into humane therapeutic centers.

William Hack Tuke, a wealthy merchant, opened one of these centers in 1797. Tuke was not a doctor, but he was motivated to change the mental health care system after the death of a close friend in an asylum. Instead of beatings, he used verbal corrections to guide his patients in a family-style

King George III

In 2003, researchers analyzed hair samples of King George III. They hoped to learn something of his bouts with a mental disorder, which was likely the hereditary disease porphyria. The disease is caused by a recessive gene, which means a person must inherit a copy of the defective gene from one or both parents in order to be affected. Because European royal families traditionally married only other royals, a high degree of inbreeding took place among them. Royal descendents suffered from a number of genetic diseases as a result.

Porphyria causes episodes of paranoia, hallucinations, and confusion. Sufferers also have seizures and other physical symptoms, including abdominal pain and vomiting. In susceptible people, porphyria attacks can be triggered by alcohol and certain medications.

Hair samples from King George III showed high levels of toxic arsenic in his system. Arsenic was an ingredient in the king's skin creams and in his wig powder. High levels of the poison were also in antimony, the medication given to the king to control his fits. Researchers wonder if the toxin triggered his attacks.

atmosphere. However, mental health care was not revolutionized overnight, and many abusive institutions lingered into the twentieth century.

TWENTIETH CENTURY

In the United States, psychiatric reform did not occur until after World War II ended in 1945. Then, medical practice shifted from separating people with mental disorders to treating them in the community. Deinstitutionalization began. By 1956, more patients were being released from mental hospitals than were being admitted.

During this time, new theories regarding prevention and treatment developed. In the 1950s, early medications successfully calmed agitated or violent patients. This made it possible for many patients with serious mental disorders to socialize, freeing them from their

Medication and Deinstitutionalization

In the mid-twentieth century, medications were not a perfect cure for people with mental disorders, but patients who used them often improved enough to be released from hospitals. However, deinstitutionalization was controversial. Unprepared patients with no work experience did not always adjust well to the outside world. Soon, community mental health care centers began, allowing patients to get help while continuing to live independent lives.

hospital rooms. Some responded so well to the medications that they were allowed to leave their institutions. Although the earliest drugs had some serious side effects, many medicines have continued to improve. Today, they provide tremendous relief for millions of people who suffer from a variety of mental disorders.

William Hogarth's painting shows a scene in Bedlam.

Mood disorders, such as depression and bipolar disorder, are common mental disorders.

COMMON MENTAL DISORDERS

There are several categories of mental disorders, including mood, anxiety, and psychotic disorders. Eating disorders and learning disorders are also classified as mental disorders. Some disorders are more common than others and affect some groups of people more often than others. Each disorder has symptoms, and some disorders have similar symptoms.

Mood Disorders

Two common mood disorders are major depressive disorder, more commonly known as depression, and bipolar disorder. Depression is characterized by symptoms including extreme sadness, loss of interest, and irritability that lasts every day for at least two weeks. Approximately 15 million adults in the United States suffer from depression. While depression ranges in severity, the illness can be debilitating, making it difficult for sufferers to get through a day. Individuals who are depressed might have suicidal thoughts or intentions. Treatments for depression include therapy and medication. The illness can usually be maintained or cured. If left

Learning Disorders and Eating Disorders

According to the *DSM-IV-TR*, learning disorders and eating disorders are classified as mental disorders. A learning disorder hinders a person's ability to learn at the same degree as his or her peers. There are many different kinds of learning disorders. A person with a learning disorder may have trouble reading, writing, or doing math.

Eating disorders affect how a person feels or behaves toward food, body weight, and body image. Common eating disorders are anorexia nervosa and bulimia nervosa. People with anorexia nervosa severely restrict the amount of food they eat and, as a result, are often dangerously underweight. People with bulimia nervosa have periods of extreme overeating and compensate by throwing up or using diuretics.

People with learning disorders and eating disorders can be helped through treatment, including medication and counseling.

untreated, however, depression can persist, remit, or grow worse.

People with bipolar disorder show variations in mood. They alternate between feeling wildly energetic and elated and deeply depressed. During manic phases, people with bipolar disorder often have racing thoughts and difficulty sleeping. They also act impulsively and exhibit poor judgment. Sometimes, highly creative people with bipolar disorder report they do their best work during manic phases. But, a reduced level of energy and symptoms of depression often follow. Sometimes a manic phase

Types of Bipolar Disorder

There are different types of bipolar disorder. All types include mania and depression. The main differences between the types are how strong the feelings of mania and depression are and when they occur. Bipolar I is characterized by extreme shifts in mood from the sadness and despair of depression to the elation and seemingly boundless energy of mania. Bipolar II is a milder form of bipolar I, and cyclothymic disorder is still milder than bipolar II.

Rapid-cycling bipolar disorder occurs when four or more extreme shifts in mood occur within a year. Some people experience such shifts within a week or a single day. This type of bipolar disorder occurs more often in women. Research has found that such rapid cycling can lead to more severe depression and a greater risk for suicide attempts.

Finally, some bipolar sufferers experience the opposite symptoms of their disorder— mania and depression—at the same time. A person can have racing thoughts and feel energetic and grandiose while also experiencing irritability, anger, and moodiness.

recurs, and sometimes it does not. Mood-stabilizing drugs such as lithium help moderate the mood swings.

SCHIZOPHRENIA

Schizophrenia is one of the most disabling psychotic disorders because sufferers have delusions and hallucinations that prevent them from functioning normally. Symptoms of the disorder usually appear in early adulthood, although evidence shows that abnormal neuronal connections in the brain are present from birth.

The disease is characterized by a variety of symptoms. Thinking is disorganized, and the ability to communicate is impaired. For people with schizophrenia, reality becomes difficult to distinguish from imagination. Sufferers withdraw socially and might appear emotionless or apathetic. Auditory, or vocal, hallucinations are common. Individuals with schizophrenia report that the voices might be entertaining, but they are most often abusive and critical. Sometimes, they even encourage violence or suicide. Patients might interpret these voices as their own thoughts, messages from God, or the telepathically transmitted thoughts of other people. Many people with schizophrenia also have visual hallucinations, which are often of a disturbing nature.

The mind of a person with schizophrenia races with thoughts that become so disorganized they impair the ability to communicate. Paranoia is a common occurrence. Sufferers often feel that someone else is controlling or interrupting their thoughts. They may imagine bizarre scenarios in which others are plotting against them. Alternately, people with schizophrenia sometimes have delusions of grandeur in which they believe they are royalty or presidents or have supernatural powers.

Although some people with schizophrenia have committed crimes while out of touch with reality, the majority of sufferers are not dangerous. Medication is effective at controlling the symptoms of schizophrenia, but most patients experience the disease either intermittently or consistently throughout their lives.

ANXIETY DISORDERS

Anxiety is an adaptive response. It keeps us attentive in potentially dangerous situations and motivates us to prepare for an uncertain future.

When anxiety gets out of control or occurs for no rational reason, then it becomes a disorder. People with anxiety disorders worry too often and feel fear in excess of what a situation would deem appropriate. Affected people often appear to be successful, but the disorder is both mentally and physically exhausting. More U.S. residents suffer from anxiety disorders than any other mental disorder. Anxiety disorders include generalized anxiety disorder (GAD), obsessive-compulsive disorder (OCD), post-traumatic stress disorder (PTSD), and phobias.

An anxiety disorder is one of the most curable disorders, with 90 percent of patients responding well to treatment. David A. Carbonell is a Chicago-area clinical psychologist specializing in anxiety disorders. He encourages anxiety sufferers to seek treatment, saying, "The effort to hide and fight the anxiety is often the most significant obstacle to recovery."[1]

National Alliance on Mental Illness

The National Alliance on Mental Illness (NAMI) works to improve the lives of people and families affected by mental disorders. According to the organization, "Mental illnesses should not be an obstacle to a full and meaningful life for persons who live with them. NAMI will advocate at all levels to ensure that all persons affected by mental illness receive the services that they need and deserve in a timely fashion."[2] NAMI has a Web site and help line with information, offers education programs and support groups, and organizes fund-raising walks.

Amber Main was diagnosed with schizophrenia during college.

A person who worries constantly might have GAD. Affected people obsess about the ways things could go wrong and imagine disastrous scenarios. Their disturbed thoughts affect them physically, almost as though a dreaded event is really happening. The stress might cause sleep problems, headaches, trembling, nausea, or lightheadedness. GAD sufferers are usually aware that their fears are groundless, but they cannot break out of their pattern of negative thinking.

Individuals with OCD have recurrent and persistent thoughts and impulses that cause anxiety and distress. Repetitive behaviors such as hand washing, checking, ordering, counting, and repeating words are activities that a person with OCD feels compelled to perform as a response to an obsession. These repetitive behaviors are performed to reduce the person's anxiety. However, they often become intrusive or inappropriate in a person's life.

Children and adults who survive traumatic experiences can develop post-traumatic stress disorder, even years after the traumatic event. People with PTSD may relive the horrible event in flashbacks or nightmares. They are easily startled and abnormally alert for danger. They may not sleep well and avoid things or people that remind them

Help for Phobias

During exposure therapy, patients with phobias are gradually exposed to anxiety-producing things in a secure environment. A person with a fear of snakes might start by thinking about snakes and then look at pictures of them. Later, the patient might see a computer simulation of a snake and then handle a realistic rubber one. Eventually, the person may choose to see a real snake in a pet store. Exposure therapy usually reduces or eliminates the fear.

Social Anxiety

Social anxiety is another type of anxiety disorder and entails an overwhelming fear of social interactions. A person with this disorder may be scared to be in public for fear of humiliation or judgment. One of the most effective therapies for people with social anxiety disorder is group therapy. People feel supported and understood in a group where everyone feels chronic social anxiety. Participants practice social skills and get feedback on their behavior. Participants often find that they do not appear as awkward to others as they feel inside.

of the event. The exact reason some people develop PTSD after an ordeal and others do not is unknown.

A phobia is an irrational fear that can consume a person. People who have phobias realize their fears are groundless, but logic does not help them feel better. For example, a person with arachnophobia has a fear of spiders and will not lose the fear when told that a particular spider is not venomous. The person cannot change his or her feelings even after gaining that knowledge.

As society tries to reach an agreement about the care of people with mental disorders, having an understanding of common disorders is imperative. Some disorders can significantly affect people's daily lives while others are quite manageable. Greater awareness can also decrease the discrimination and stigma that are linked to mental disorders. ⌐

June Moss, right, visited with a veteran friend in 2008. Moss served in Iraq in 2003 and suffers from post-traumatic stress disorder.

Di'Anna Malone leads a support group for people who have a family member with a mental disorder.

OVERCOMING STIGMA

eople who are different from mainstream society are sometimes stigmatized. They may suffer discrimination in housing, employment, and education. They may be ignored or treated with suspicion or disdain.

In the United States, groups that have historically faced stigma include women, ethnic groups, sexual minorities, the economically disadvantaged, and people with mental disorders. During the 1960s, these groups began demanding equal rights. As a result, societal attitudes and behavior began to change. Although members of disadvantaged groups still face discrimination, many are now protected by laws.

Unique Challenges

However, stigma continues to be a significant barrier for people with mental disorders. Employers are reluctant to hire them, and landlords are not eager to rent to them. These realities can leave people with mental disorders struggling to meet their basic needs. Even friends and family members can pull away when someone reveals that he or she is battling a mental disorder. This can leave the sufferer without needed social interaction, friendship, love, and support.

Discrimination Causes Stress

Members of underrepresented ethnic groups and sexual minorities may experience chronic stress due to discrimination. The anticipation of rejection causes anxiety, even if the feared rebuff never occurs. Of course, actual attacks—verbal or physical—are sources of extreme distress. This stress impacts mental health in minority communities, increasing the incidence of anxiety in people of color.

Joyce Burland is the national director of the Education, Training, and Peer Support Center at the National Alliance on Mental Illness. She spoke about the situation faced by families with a member who has a mental disorder:

> *Families say this is the only illness in the world where you don't get a covered dish. People don't call, don't inquire. The cultural understanding of mental illness is either that it's their fault for getting ill, or it's the fault of their family.* [1]

Because of these unfortunate beliefs, many families dealing with a mental disorder conceal their problem or feel unwarranted shame.

Paul Appelbaum is a professor in Columbia University's Department of Psychiatry. He believes many people fear others with mental disorders will commit crimes and act dangerously. Appelbaum believes these fears are exaggerated and that this focus should instead be placed on treatment:

> *We are being misled by our own fears. We ought to be concerned about providing good treatment and helping people lead fulfilling lives, not obsessed with protecting ourselves from phantom threats that appear to be unrelated to mental illness.* [2]

According to a 2007 study, almost one-third of parents surveyed would prefer that their child not become friends with a child suffering from depression or attention-deficit/ hyperactivity disorder (ADHD). Twenty percent of these parents would not even want such a child to live next door. The parents of children with mental disorders are often blamed for their children's disorders and are sometimes rumored to be abusive. Although abuse can result in mental disorders, genetic causes have

Stigma at an Extreme

During World War II, stigmatization of people with mental disorders resulted in the deaths of nearly 200,000 patients in Europe. Between 1933 and 1945, Adolf Hitler led the authoritarian Nazi Party that ruled Germany. Hitler's goal was to create a pure form of the German race by eliminating the people he thought were undesirable. This included people with mental disorders.

In September 1939, Hitler signed a decree requiring physicians to euthanize, or kill, incurable mental patients without the consent of their families. Authorities at hospitals and mental institutions were ordered to list their patients who were unable to work due to mental disorders, who spent five years in an asylum, or who were criminally insane. Teams of psychiatrists then decided who lived and who died. Between 1939 and 1941, 73,000 adults and children who were hospital patients were put to death.

During a secret meeting in 1942, institute directors were informed of a new policy. Beginning in 1943, incurable patients were put on the E-diet, a fat-free, vitamin-free starvation ration composed mostly of boiled vegetables. Although some nurses tried to sneak patients food, 110,000 of them starved to death. In total, approximately 183,000 psychiatric patients were killed.

In May 2004, the National Alliance for the Mentally Ill held Walk for the Mind to bring attention to Mental Health Awareness Month.

been discovered. Bipolar disorder and schizophrenia are two mental disorders that can be passed down through genes.

Attitudes of young adults toward others with mental disorders also reflect a general lack of understanding. Although one person out of five between the ages of 18 and 24 reports having a mental disorder, only around one person out of four in this age group believes that people who experience mental disorders can recover.

Experts estimate that two out of every three people with mental disorders do not receive the help they need. They may not seek out treatment because they fear being labeled as crazy or because they are unaware of the illnesses and their symptoms. The symptoms of children can be easily overlooked or mistaken for difficult developmental phases. At the same time, the stakes of ignoring a mental disorder are high. People with depression, bipolar disorder, or schizophrenia are at high risk for suicide. In fact, approximately 70 percent of teens who commit suicide suffered from a treatable mental disorder.

ANTIDISCRIMINATION ACTS

In 1990, legislation passed that safeguarded many rights of people with mental disorders. The Americans with Disabilities Act (ADA) prevents discrimination against people with mental disorders in employment, transportation, accommodation at hotels, and other public services. For example, at work, a person with a mental disorder should have access to paid or unpaid leave for hospitalization, rearrangement of work schedules to allow for meetings with psychiatrists, and extra supervision by managers. A person with a mental disorder must still meet the education and experience qualifications needed to do the job. Also, retaining that employee cannot cause undue hardship to the employer.

In interviews, potential employers are not allowed to ask if a person has a mental disorder or has any history of psychiatric treatment. Employers are allowed to determine if a potential employee is capable of showing up to work regularly, handling job stresses professionally, and getting along with coworkers.

Mental Disorders, Alcohol, and Suicide

Most people with mental disorders do not commit suicide. However, depression, bipolar disorder, and schizophrenia are mental disorders that increase the risk of suicide. Alcohol use by people with these disorders compounds the problem. Blood tests of suicide victims reveal that 40 to 60 percent of them were intoxicated at the times of their deaths.

In 1968, the Fair Housing Act outlawed discrimination on the basis of race, religion, and disability. Yet, housing continues to be problematic. Landlords can still legally turn away an individual who may be disruptive, destructive, or dangerous. However, if a person with a mental disorder thinks a landlord turned him or her away because of a disability, proving discrimination can be difficult.

Furthermore, communities are not always welcoming to people with mental disorders. A licensed group home is a residential facility that houses and cares for people with disabilities. When mental health care professionals try to open group homes, neighborhood associations frequently oppose them. A 2008 U.S. Department of Health survey found that 12 percent of adults would not want to live next door to someone who has a mental disorder. This percentage increased from 8 percent in 1994.

REDUCING STIGMA

Protection and Advocacy for Individuals with Mental Illness (PAIMI) is a patient advocate group that supports people with mental disorders in a variety of settings, including prisons, homeless shelters, and group homes.

Advocates blame the media for creating skewed perceptions of people with mental disorders. In suspense movies, such people are often portrayed as savages who use their intellect only to plan attacks. PAIMI recommends that people who are offended by media portrayals contact studios and register polite complaints.

PAIMI also suggests that all people monitor their language, avoiding negative terms for people with mental disorders. They prefer terms that emphasize

Mental Health Parity Act

At one time, health insurance companies set lower limits on mental health benefits than they did on physical health benefits. This meant that people had less coverage for mental disorders than for physical disorders and would have to come up with more money to pay for their mental health care. The Mental Health Parity Act of 1996 is the federal law that changed that.

the person instead of the disorder. Referring to a person diagnosed with schizophrenia as a "person with schizophrenia" is better than calling him or her a "schizophrenic." The term "mental disorder" is often substituted for "mental illness." Some people prefer the term "brain disease" in order to emphasize similarities between mental and physical diseases. Patient advocates work to allow people with mental disorders to be treated with respect. ⌐

President George H. W. Bush signed the Americans with Disabilities Act in 1990.

Former director general of the World Health Organization, Gro Harlem Brundtland, discussed public health, including mental health, in 2001.

IMPACT OF MENTAL DISORDERS

The World Health Organization (WHO) is the division of the United Nations that works to improve public health worldwide. To identify diseases that pose the biggest problems to society, WHO uses the disability-adjusted life year

(DALY) system. In the DALY system, years of life lost because of early death from disease are counted together with years of poor health. The total number of lost and limited years reveals the impact of each disease. The 2000 Global Burden of Disease study looked at all diseases and used the DALY system to quantify the burden that each one places on society.

The DALY results for mental disorders were startling. The strain caused by major depression was equal to that of blindness or paraplegia. The hallucinations and delusions of schizophrenia were on par with quadriplegia. All mental disorders together accounted for 12 percent of the total burden of disease in developed countries.

SEUNG-HUI CHO

Mental disorders have a greater influence on society than many people realize. When people suffer from physical diseases, they often tell their friends and family, who are supportive during a difficult time. Mental disorders are too often thought of as private matters. Sufferers may keep the issue to themselves. They are left without emotional support, and the public is unaware of the scope of the problem.

In 2002, Tallahassee, Florida, officials spoke about the negative effects that untreated mental disorders can have on the community.

The impact of untreated mental disorders can be tragic. In 2007, Virginia Tech student Seung-Hui Cho carried off well-planned murders at the college. Cho entered a building and chained the doors shut before shooting almost 50 people and killing himself. In 2005, Cho had undergone a court-ordered psychiatric evaluation and was diagnosed with a nonspecific mood disorder. He was released with the suggestion he continue with outpatient counseling, but he was not prescribed any medication. The shooting showed society a worst-case scenario for an untreated mental disorder.

Perception of Violence

One reason people with mental disorders face stigma is because much of the public mistakenly believes that people with mental disorders are violent. The majority of people with mental disorders, especially those who receive treatment, are not violent.

Unfortunately, it is not possible to accurately predict which patients will become violent, but psychiatrists use their knowledge and health care guidelines to make as accurate assessments, diagnoses, and treatment plans as possible.

Family Members and Caregivers

A mental disorder also impacts caregivers and family members. When a member of a family has a mental disorder, the entire family is put under tremendous strain. For one, providing support demands time and attention, and treatment can be costly. Also, those unfamiliar with a person diagnosed with a mental disorder might not understand his or her behavior, so the family might isolate themselves or keep the illness a secret. Such reactions cause additional stress. Relatives may have trouble coping with all the pressure. They might feel guilty or blame each other for causing the condition or handling it badly.

Parents of a child with a mental disorder go through a long-term grief process not unlike that following a death. The dreams—and even basic expectations—they had for their child may not come true. A mother who once attended her son's soccer games now attends meetings with his therapist instead. A father who once hoped his daughter would get into a good college now hopes that she will get out of bed. Parents mourn the loss of their dreams even though their children are still alive.

In an article for the National Mental Health Association, Vicki Koenig, PhD, addressed affected families, saying, "The diagnosis of mental illness is much like a physical diagnosis such as cancer, MS, etc. Therefore, some of the emotions that you may be experiencing are about loss and grief."[1] Koenig emphasizes that such families need a great deal of external support from friends, extended family, or support groups. One helpful idea to remember is that mental disorders are not necessarily life

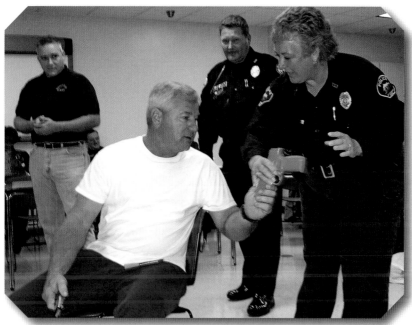

At a 2007 training program, Georgia police officers learned to identify and handle people with mental disorders who may act violently.

sentences. Some brain disorders will require long-term care, but many respond well to treatment and are manageable.

Children of people with mental disorders particularly face extreme hardship. They cannot escape from the parent's rage, anxiety, or irrationality but do not have the resources to care for themselves. These children are at high risk for abuse and neglect, especially if the parent is also a

substance abuser. These children may try to make
things right by being as perfect as possible. They
often take on responsibilities outside their role,
such as cooking and cleaning, in order to make the
household function. Others may adopt a parent's
odd behavior or become wild and rebellious. Such
children often lack knowledge of basic hygiene
and are not accepted because they go to school
looking and smelling dirty. They may suffer from
malnutrition or have untreated injuries inflicted
by the parent. Teachers and classmates can contact
social services and report these situations to help
such children get the care and attention they need.

Several mental disorders have genetic
components. The stress of taking care of a family
member who has a mental disorder can trigger
the symptoms of a mental disorder in susceptible
individuals. Environmental factors, including
traumatic experiences, can also trigger a mental
disorder. Since life with a relative with a mental
disorder can be stressful and challenging, more than
one family member may develop a mental disorder.
Unrelated caregivers who must be on constant alert
around a volatile person are at risk for developing
anxiety disorders.

To prevent burnout, caregivers must schedule time to relax and socialize with their friends. Marking plans on the calendar makes them more likely to occur. Yet, some caregivers have a tendency not to follow through with plans due to their patients' behavior. Scheduling backup care is essential to give caregivers the rest they need.

FINANCIAL COSTS OF MENTAL DISORDERS

In 2002, mental disorders cost the United States approximately $317 billion. This figure includes the costs of treatment, subsidized

Risk Factors for Developing Schizophrenia

Schizophrenia is a serious mental disorder characterized by frightening hallucinations and delusions. Affected people may hear voices that do not really exist, or they may imagine that others are plotting against them. Schizophrenia affects approximately 1 in every 100 people. Mutations in several different genes contribute to schizophrenia, but environmental components also contribute to the disease.

Relatives of people with schizophrenia are at increased risk of developing it themselves. Other factors that increase the likelihood of developing schizophrenia, although only slight, include being born in winter, having poor health during childhood, having an older father, and living in an urban area. The health of a mother during pregnancy also affects a baby's chance of developing schizophrenia later in life. Breastfeeding lowers risk, but if the pregnant woman drinks alcohol, acquires certain infections, or is very overweight, the risk to the baby increases. Marijuana use by genetically vulnerable individuals increases their odds of developing schizophrenia, but it does not have this effect on people who are not genetically vulnerable.

housing, disability and social security payments, and lost productivity of workers. This estimate does not include income lost by people with mental disorders who become homeless or die young. The figure also leaves out the cost of imprisoning those with mental disorders, which is significant because criminals with mental disorders make up 22 percent of prisoners in U.S. jails.

Although treatment and medication for people with mental disorders may be initially expensive, they save money over time. Medication keeps patients employed and living independently, rather than housed in expensive institutions. Treating a person with schizophrenia with the medication clozapine saves approximately $23,000 per year because of the decreased need for hospitalization.

To Reduce Anxiety

There are several methods caregivers can take to reduce anxiety:

- Get regular aerobic exercise.
- Stretch or do yoga.
- Schedule relaxing activities, especially with friends.
- Drop out of unsatisfying clubs and organizations.
- Ask others to help with tasks.

A caregiver explains the medication schedule a patient will follow.

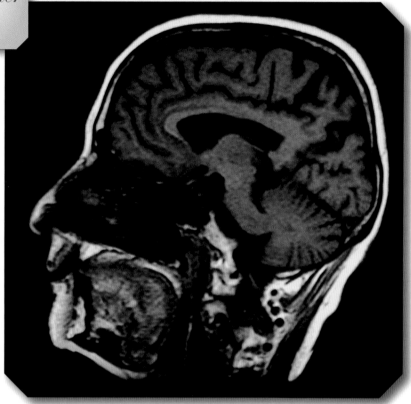

Chemical imbalances in the brain can lead to a mental disorder.

CAUSES, PREVENTION, AND TREATMENT

People acquire mental disorders for many reasons. Some mental disorders are caused by biochemical imbalances in the brain. Neurons, specialized communication cells in the nervous system, release neurotransmitters to send signals throughout the brain and spinal cord. If the wrong amount of a neurotransmitter is released, a person can experience unhealthy changes in mood or lose the ability to focus. For example, some cases of depression are associated with low levels of the neurotransmitter serotonin.

Other mental disorders may result from the environment or a predisposition. These risk factors make it more likely that a person will develop a mental disorder, but they do not guarantee it. There are three types of risk factors: biological, psychological, and environmental.

Biological Risk Factors

Biological risk factors include genetic predispositions to certain disorders, such as anxiety and depression. These illnesses can be passed down through family. Infectious diseases are also biological risk factors, since some microorganisms can cause mental disorders. For example, pregnant women who are infected by influenza have a higher risk of having children

Common Risk Factors

Several common risk factors for mental disorders include:
- low birth weight
- chronic physical illness
- below-average intelligence
- paternal criminality
- maternal mental disorder
- being in foster care
- attending inadequate schools
- being a victim of violence

who later develop schizophrenia. Severe mental, behavioral, and emotional dysfunction is one of the effects of late stage syphilis, a sexually transmitted disease.

Stress Damages Children's Brains

Children of parents with high levels of stress are more likely to be anxious or depressed than those of parents with low levels of stress. Researchers have surmised that parents take out their stress on their children, causing their kids to feel similarly stressed. The risk is increased for those who carry a form of a gene known to make people sensitive to stress. Affected children tend to act very shy.

Severe stress and trauma can damage even the physical structure of a young brain. The hippocampus is a region in the brain that functions in memory and emotion. It has been found to be smaller in children diagnosed with post-traumatic stress disorder (PTSD) due to abuse, loss, or a violent environment. This brain damage makes them inattentive and hyperactive. Such children can show stress-induced brain damage even if they have no genetic predisposition to sensitivity to stress.

"We're not talking about the stress of doing your homework or fighting with your dad," said child psychiatrist Victor Carrion, who is affiliated with Lucile Packard Children's Hospital in Palo Alto, California. "We're talking about traumatic stress. These kids feel like they're stuck in the middle of a street with a truck barreling down at them."[1]

Researchers are working to identify mutations in genes that affect brain functioning, so efforts at prevention can target susceptible individuals. Risk assessments will be more accurate once scientists can identify the specific genes that are associated with each disorder.

An identical twin of a person with schizophrenia has approximately a 50 percent chance of developing the disorder, even when raised apart from his or her twin. This indicates that the disease has a genetic component. In 2006, researchers found the first genes that increased the risk of schizophrenia. One gene they found is called neuregulin 1, and it works at synapses—spots where one nerve cell communicates with the next. People who have a defective version of the gene are not doomed to get schizophrenia, but they do have a higher risk of developing the disorder.

Experts recommend that people with family histories of schizophrenia take extra measures for prevention. These include living in a rural area and avoiding marijuana. Studies show that stress should be minimized, since it has been shown to damage children's developing brains. Though these suggestions may lower the risk of developing the mental disorder, experts believe more research is needed to know for sure.

Ethicists have voiced concern about the ramifications of studies that reveal genetic predispositions to diseases. Such information will be invaluable in designing effective treatments, but, if it became public, it could be misused. Insurance companies might choose not to insure susceptible

Mental Health Care Professionals

A variety of professionals provide mental health care. Psychiatrists are medical doctors with additional psychiatric training, so they can prescribe medication. They can also perform examinations to rule out possible physical causes for problems. Psychologists are not medical doctors, although many have PhDs, or doctoral degrees. They primarily do counseling and therapy, but they cannot prescribe medications. Psychoanalysts can be psychiatrists or psychologists. They analyze patients, meaning that they help them explore unconscious motivations for their behavior.

people. A person known to carry the gene for a mental disorder might have trouble getting a job that requires a security clearance. How much personal genetic information should be obtained and who should have access to it are ongoing topics of debate.

PSYCHOLOGICAL AND ENVIRONMENTAL RISK FACTORS

Biological risk factors are not alone in contributing to the development of a mental disorder. Psychological and environmental conditions, which usually affect home life, also have a significant effect. They include substance abuse, marital conflict, having large numbers of children, and low income. Biological predispositions might explain why some people in high-risk situations develop mental disorders while others do not.

When a traumatic event affects a large group of people, some individuals recover better than others.

This may be due to resilience, or resistance to stress. Factors that might strengthen resilience are happy childhoods, stable home lives, sufficient economic resources, and healthy lifestyles. Because resilience has to do with healthy people, it is inherently more difficult to study than factors that increase the odds of illness.

Mental health professionals attempt to differentiate between risk factors that cannot be changed, such as genetic ones, and those that can, such as social support networks. Therapists try to focus on those areas they can improve. For example, a school psychologist probably will not be able to alter dysfunctional family dynamics. However, he or she can change a student's classroom assignment or increase therapy sessions.

Treatment of Mental Disorders

Treatment methods for mental disorders can be generally divided into two categories: pharmacologic and psychotherapeutic. Pharmacologic treatments include medicine or psychotropic drugs. But these methods do not always work. Sometimes people with severe and chronic depression are not helped with medicine. In these cases, a different type

Talk therapy is often helpful for a person experiencing a mental disorder.

of treatment, electroshock therapy, is required. Electroshock therapy is a medical procedure that electrically induces seizures in anesthetized patients to relieve symptoms of depression. Psychotherapeutic treatments focus on thoughts, feelings, and behaviors. They encompass a wide range of talk therapies, hypnosis, and behavior therapy. Pharmacologic and psychotherapeutic treatments are usually more effective when used together than by themselves.

During most modern talk therapies, patients discuss their problems with therapists who try to help them develop healthier coping strategies. Therapists also help patients by correcting faulty logic that causes distress. For example, a mother told her therapist that her children did not love her. If they loved her, she reasoned, they would clean their rooms to make her happy. The therapist helped the mother see that this logic was not necessarily correct. Children might just be untidy because of their nature, not because of their feelings toward their mother.

Different types of medications are available to treat people with mental disorders. Those suffering from depression often benefit from serotonin reuptake inhibitors. These medications prevent the brain's natural reuptake, or absorption, of the neurotransmitter serotonin after

Toxoplasma and Schizophrenia

Scientists have discovered that *Toxoplasma gondii*, a parasite transmitted in cat feces, may trigger the development of schizophrenia and bipolar disorder. Cats become infected with the parasite by eating infected rodents or small animals. In humans, the infection can cause the brain to make dopamine, which changes a person's mood and behavior. All schizophrenia drugs in use today affect dopamine production, suggesting that the parasite's effect is real. Experiments are under way to treat people with schizophrenia for *Toxoplasma* infection, on the chance that an infection is the root cause of their illness.

Side Effects

Medications are often used in the treatment of mental disorders. The drugs can cause side effects in some patients and not in others. Some antipsychotics can cause akathisia, which is a sense of unease or restlessness that may be almost unnoticed by some patients. In other patients, akathisia can be severe, causing anxiety or absolute terror. Other medications can cause sedation, tremors, weight gain, and sexual dysfunction.

it has been released in the brain's synapses. Having serotonin remain longer in the brain can bring the level of that neurotransmitter back to normal, alleviating the depression.

Other classes of drugs include antipsychotic drugs used to treat schizophrenia, mood stabilizers for bipolar disorder, and anti-anxiety drugs. Prescription drugs can help people feel like themselves again, but some have unhealthy side effects. Certain medications might strain the liver or kidneys, so they should be taken only under the guidance of a physician.

Psychiatrists discourage patients from purchasing medications over the Internet because online pharmaceuticals may be counterfeit or past their expiration date. Even more important, patients need to have relationships with doctors who know and care about them. ⌐

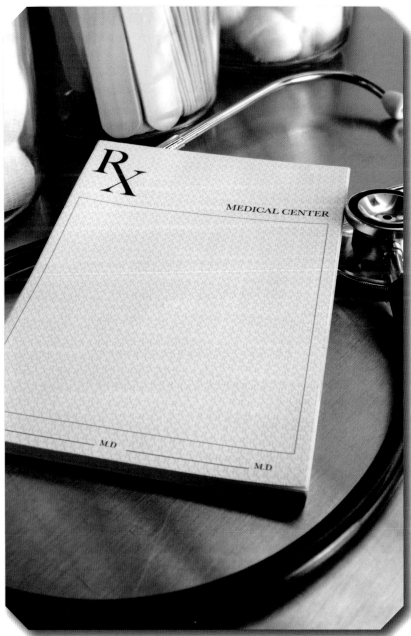

A doctor can prescribe medication to treat a patient with a mental disorder.

Arlecia Hickman is an inmate in the mental health unit at a Cleveland, Ohio, jail.

MENTAL DISORDERS
AND THE LAW

The criminal justice system is designed to balance the rights of individuals with the rights of society. In cases where defendants with mental disorders received unusually long sentences, the system seems to have shifted toward protecting society at the expense of individual rights. In other instances, patients with mental disorders who have committed murders have been pronounced cured and released into society, only to kill again. Their rights clearly took precedence over the safety of society. Because no one can predict with total accuracy which inmates will offend again, the system is naturally imperfect. It relies on the experience and the intuition of the people who make up the criminal justice system.

When a person with an apparent mental disorder enters the criminal justice system, he or she can be ordered by a judge to undergo a psychiatric evaluation. This is to determine whether the defendant is mentally competent to participate in his or her defense. It is also to determine if the defendant understood that his or her actions were illegal and if the defendant could distinguish right from wrong at the time of the crime.

A person unable to make this distinction will probably not be able to aid his attorney or understand the trial proceedings. In such cases, the Due Process Clause of the Fourteenth Amendment will prohibit criminal prosecution. The defendant will not be considered competent to stand trial and instead will receive treatment in a mental institution. He or she might recover enough to stand trial later.

In the 1986 case *Ford v. Wainwright*, the U.S. Supreme Court banned the execution of the criminally insane. But the debate continues on how ill a person must be to be considered exempt from responsibility for his or her actions.

Forced Medication Allowed

In the 2003 case *Sell v. United States*, the U.S. Supreme Court ruled it was legal to forcibly medicate a defendant with a mental disorder in order to make that person competent

An Insanity Plea

In the early 1980s, John Hinckley Jr. was obsessed with actress Jodie Foster. He followed the young woman to her residence at Yale University and put notes in her mailbox. He even telephoned her a few times. He obsessed about ways to gain her attention and decided that assassinating a president would work best. In his deluded thinking, this would impress the movie star and make her love him.

On March 30, 1981, Hinckley fired six shots at President Ronald Reagan. The president was hit, but he survived. A secret service agent, a police officer, and Press Secretary James Brady were also wounded. Hinckley called his assassination attempt "the greatest love offering in the history of the world."[1]

In court, Hinckley was found not guilty by reason of insanity and, as of 2009, remained in a mental hospital. As a result of his case, legislators began to discuss the requirements of an insanity plea. A number of states changed their laws regarding the insanity defense, making it much more difficult to use.

to stand trial. This ruling does not apply to all defendants with mental disorders, however. Those who are already being treated in secured institutions might never go to trial.

In order to forcibly medicate a defendant for trial, the government has to find that the case is important enough to warrant a trial. Then, the prescribed medication must be shown to be effective, necessary, and medically appropriate. If no less invasive means will work, a defendant can be treated with antipsychotic medications against his or her will.

People who disagree with this ruling argue that taking medication is not in the best interests of a patient if the result is a possible conviction or even execution. For this reason, some doctors see forcible medication of defendants as a violation of their Hippocratic oath. Under this oath, physicians have sworn to do no harm to their patients.

Medication Overruled

Wayne Moruzin was charged with robbing a New Jersey bank in 2005, but, as of 2009, he will not be going to trial any time soon. Moruzin hallucinates and is paranoid and delusional; he is not competent to stand trial. To make him fit for trial, prosecutors wanted to force him to take injections of Haldol, an antipsychotic drug. Moruzin refused, and the judge agreed. The judge stated that Moruzin is not violent or suicidal, and the drug he would take could have serious side effects. Haldol makes patients involuntarily grimace and tremble, which could put off jurors and compromise an individual's ability to receive a fair trial.

Mental health supporters attended a rally in Jackson, Mississippi, in 2004.

The Insanity Defense

Contrary to popular opinion, the insanity defense is not an easy or likely way for criminals to be absolved of responsibility for their crimes. It is used in only 1 percent of trials and successful only approximately 25 percent of the time. Depending on the U.S. state, the insanity defense can take several forms. A defendant can be found not guilty by reason of insanity or guilty but mentally ill.

The practical outcome of the difference lies in sentencing. People found not guilty by reason of insanity are locked in mental hospitals. A patient whose condition improved might be released if the committing court reexamined the case and mental health professionals recommended it. Continued freedom would depend on the patient following a set of conditions, such as taking medication, meeting with a therapist, and avoiding alcohol and drugs.

Defendants who receive a verdict of guilty but mentally ill may have to serve their entire sentences in jail. They are supposed to receive mental health care in prison, but many prisons are so understaffed that patients wait weeks or months for a meeting with a therapist. The quality of mental health care in a prison setting is generally much poorer than that available in a mental institution. After an individual satisfies the sentence, he or she enters the parole system. The granting and conditions of parole are established by the parole board in each state.

A lawyer would never advise a client to pretend to be insane as a strategy. Criminals with mental disorders often receive longer sentences than others who have committed similar crimes. This is due, in part, to the Supreme Court's 2005 decision in *United*

Supermax Prisons

People with mental disorders usually do not adjust well to prison. They often are not capable of remembering and following prison regulations, so they get punished repeatedly. In the past, such inmates were isolated and confined in separate facilities called Supermax prisons. Here, prisoners often had psychological breakdowns and mutilated themselves or attempted suicide. Attorney David Fathi of the American Civil Liberties Union's National Prison Project said, "Courts have previously recognized that housing the seriously mentally ill in this type of environment amounts to torture."[2] The placement of prisoners with mental disorders in Supermax prisons has since been ruled unconstitutional.

States v. Booker. This ruling gave judges more leeway to increase sentences of defendants in federal crimes. Some judges have taken advantage of the opportunity, passing extremely long sentences for defendants with mental disorders in particular. This is especially so when the crime was particularly heinous or the judge thinks the person is likely to offend again. Human rights advocates argue that giving longer sentences to people with mental disorders is discriminatory and unfair. They argue that standard sentences should be followed by hospitalization, if needed.

Former First Lady Rosalynn Carter and her husband, President Jimmy Carter, are two of these advocates. They founded the Carter Center, a human rights organization working to protect the rights of those with mental disorders in the criminal justice system. Mrs. Carter said:

Children and mentally ill individuals cannot fully participate in their defense or understand the nature and consequences of the legal proceedings. They also make poor witnesses at trials, leading the jury to sometimes misunderstand and punish the behavior they observe during trial.[3]

OUTPATIENT COMMITMENT

Outpatient commitment is a court order that requires a patient with a mental disorder who has committed a crime and is at high risk for reoffending to comply with mental health treatment while living independently. Originally, outpatient commitment was intended as a benevolent alternative to treatment in a secured setting, but it has become controversial. Some outpatients argue that the justice system has no right to force them to take medication against their will or make them attend meetings with psychiatrists. Advocates for people with mental disorders see outpatient commitment as a poor, low-budget substitute for better, more expensive individualized services.

Supporters of outpatient commitment feel that it stops a dangerous cycle often seen in people with mental disorders. Patients frequently stop taking their medication, experience a decline in mental health, and are returned to hospitals. By mandating that these patients check in with doctors, this cycle may be broken. Laws vary between states, but usually patients can be compelled to take medication only if they have a history of violence or self-destructive behavior. ⌐

*Many supporters of outpatient commitment see counseling
as a useful tool for patients.*

In 2004, First Lady of Wisconsin Jessica Doyle spoke in support of a bill
that would help patients with mental disorders.

PATIENT RIGHTS

People with mental disorders have not
always had the same rights as people
without mental disorders. However, current
legal guidelines allow mental patients the most
freedom possible. In some cases, this means living

independently and seeing a therapist regularly. Other individuals might live in supervised group homes or institutions. People with mental disorders who are institutionalized are free to socialize and move about their facilities as long as they are not violent or suicidal.

FORCED MEDICATION

As part of a court-ordered treatment plan, a person can be legally ordered to take medication. Those in favor of this practice argue that medication allows patients with mental disorders to live independently, keep jobs, and maintain relationships with loved ones. However, some of these drugs can have unpleasant and unhealthy side effects. Some individuals stop taking their medication to avoid its side effects and so experience a return of their symptoms. These patients may feel as though they are in a no-win situation.

Some patients' rights advocates say patients are entitled to refuse medication. Many psychiatrists

Agreement in Treatment

Treatment of people with mental disorders in the United States is in line with a human rights resolution adopted by the United Nations General Assembly on December 17, 1991. The resolution details the specific human rights of mental patients and requires their humane and dignified treatment.

disagree, believing that people with serious mental
disorders may not have the capability to make
the best decisions for themselves. Both sides in
the debate see the issue as one of freedom. Judi
Chamberlin, senior associate of the National
Empowerment Center in Lawrence, Massachusetts,
is a legal rights advocate. She said, "The question
might better be framed as, 'Should psychiatrists
be able to define people as "patients" against
their will?'"[1] Chamberlin believes services such as
counseling and job placement are most helpful
and that funding should go toward these programs
because "every dollar spent on surveillance and
control [to force patients to take medicine] is a
dollar that is not available to fund services."[2]

E. Fuller Torrey, president of the Treatment
Advocacy Center in Arlington, Virginia, disagrees.
Torrey believes that many people with mental
disorders do not understand that they are ill, so they
will not seek treatment:

> *On humane grounds alone, is it fair to leave those who are*
> *not aware of their own illness living in the streets and eating*
> *out of garbage cans, as over 25 percent of the population*
> *with severe mental illnesses do?[3]*

Members of Congress showed support for mental health legislation during a rally in 2008.

In this view, the patients' right to recover overrides their right to refuse treatment.

Involuntary Commitment

Individuals with mental disorders most often come in conflict with their communities when they lack family members or social workers to aid with housing, counseling, and job placement. Without a support system, these individuals are at risk for becoming homeless.

Involuntary commitment is the confinement of a person in a mental hospital against his or her will. Currently, it can be enforced only if a patient is a danger to himself or herself or others, but this was not always the case. In the United States, a person could once be certified as mentally ill at the request of a family member and a physician. Although this system did identify many people in need, it was easily misused. Powerful people could make those less powerful disappear by certifying them as insane.

In the past, husbands sometimes used institutionalization to get rid of their wives, especially in conservative communities where divorce was not an option. This problem became common enough that laws were written to prevent it. The first of these laws was passed in 1874 in Maine.

In the 1930s, Maine legislator Gail Laughlin sponsored a bill that penalized husbands who lied in order to commit their wives. As late as the 1960s, a woman who did not conform to the traditional role of housewife—that is, who argued with her husband or did not clean—could be committed to a mental hospital. Today, federal law mandates court hearings and psychiatric evaluations to prevent healthy people from being wrongly institutionalized.

RIGHTS OF PATIENTS OUTSIDE INSTITUTIONS

In 1975, the U.S. Supreme Court ruled in *O'Connor v. Donaldson* that individuals with mental disorders who pose no risk to themselves or others could not be forced into institutions. Some states make exceptions for people who are unable to care for themselves. Homeless people with mental disorders may fall into this category and can find shelter in treatment centers.

Wyatt v. Stickney

In 1970, an exposé of the horrendous living conditions at Bryce State Hospital in Tuscaloosa, Alabama, shocked the public. Bryce was known as a dumping ground for unwanted people, where those with mental disorders remained out of public sight. Its wards were so crowded that beds touched. In addition, juvenile delinquents who were not diagnosed with a mental disorder could be court-ordered to go to the hospital if they failed to adjust to foster care or group homes. Fifteen-year-old Ricky Wyatt was one of these juvenile delinquents, and the landmark court case *Wyatt v. Stickney* was filed on his behalf.

Wyatt was admitted into Bryce in 1969. In 1970, Wyatt and his guardian became involved in a lawsuit against Bryce State Hospital. Wyatt told the court of the terrible living conditions at Bryce. He was locked in a dark cell that had no bed and was forced to sleep on the damp floor. Patients there received electroshock therapy as punishment and were kept sedated most of the time. Wyatt was released from Bryce State Hospital in 1973.

The case was not closed until 2003, when a judge finally agreed that the institution was not treating its patients with dignity. The *Wyatt v. Stickney* ruling set minimum standards for patient care and treatment in all U.S. institutions.

RIGHTS OF PATIENTS IN INSTITUTIONS

In order to be treated in secured settings, people with mental disorders must pose a real danger to themselves or society. Nonviolent patients are treated in the least restrictive settings possible, which usually means they live independently or in group homes and receive care in their own communities. For a nonviolent person with a mental disorder to be institutionalized, he or she would have to be incapable of the most basic self-care. An example would be a patient who becomes catatonic and loses the ability to move or feed himself or herself.

In the United States, many people voluntarily admit themselves to psychiatric hospitals on the advice of their physicians. It is common for a psychiatric hospital stay to last no more than 72 hours. During this time, the patient is evaluated and then either released or advised to admit himself or herself voluntarily. Voluntary commitments for longer periods of time are based on need, ability to pay, and health insurance. These stays are generally short, often only a few weeks. This is especially true since economic factors have forced health insurance companies to limit benefits. Intensive treatment in a facility is usually followed by outpatient care.

One of the foremost rights of patients in mental hospitals is the right to treatment. This right prevents institutions from becoming warehouses for those with mental disorders and ensures that patients have a genuine expectation of release. Patients have the right to be kept safe from assaults by other patients and staff members. They have the right not to be restrained—unless they are violent. Institutionalized patients do have the right to refuse medication, but psychiatrists in some states may request the court to order forced medication if absolutely necessary.

Institutionalized patients also have rights that help make them feel as independent as possible. They have the right to receive visitors, make phone calls, send and receive mail, and vote. They may keep their personal belongings, with the exception of banned materials such as drugs and weapons. Perhaps most

O'Connor v. Donaldson

In the 1975 U.S. Supreme Court case *O'Connor v. Donaldson*, Kenneth Donaldson sued the mental hospital that had kept him for 15 years against his will. The court found that involuntary treatment was a violation of Donaldson's civil rights, and the law was changed. Prior to this case, patients with mental disorders could be confined even if they were nonviolent.

important, patients have the right to be partners with their doctors in their treatment process. They may see their own files, discuss their long-term treatment options, and help make decisions about their future. Any patient who believes his or her rights have been violated may file a grievance and seek legal representation. ⌁

In 1999, President Bill Clinton spoke at the White House Conference on Mental Health.

Chapter 9

SUMNER MENTAL HEALTH CENTER
North Campus — 15 Industrial Avenue

Many communities across the United States have mental health care facilities such as this one in Wellington, Kansas.

Recovery and Empowerment

atients with even the most serious mental disorders may recover completely. Others may face a lifetime of treatment and hospitalization. What are the key differences between patients who recover and those who do not? Genetics is a factor, but genes cannot be altered. Mental health care practitioners look for factors they can change in order to foster recovery.

Social support has proven beneficial for long-term recovery. Patients who feel someone—even a low-level hospital staff member—has faith in them report more successful treatment. Daniel Fisher, a psychiatrist who recovered from schizophrenia, explained the importance of feeling supported:

> *Clients we have interviewed describe this relationship as being with "a person who believed in me." This attitude is conveyed through direct, open, and spontaneous communication, a way of interacting that seems to be "trained out" of many professionals. Nearly every one of these mental health consumers concurred that they received their best help from the least trained staff in hospitals.[1]*

The World Health Organization (WHO) completed studies in 1979 and in 1992 that compared recovery rates for schizophrenia between developed and developing nations. Recovery rates in the developing nations were approximately twice as high as those in the developed nations. Treatment in developing nations emphasized social support, so patients were kept in contact with numerous caring people. In developed countries, clients were largely cut off from former social networks when they were admitted to mental hospitals.

Being labeled as a person with a mental disorder automatically causes some stigma and disconnection from society. But the stigma can also come from within. Patients may have trouble accepting themselves following a diagnosis. They may assume they are somehow less worthy than those without a mental disorder and feel sentenced to a life with fewer

Support Groups

Support groups are often a good resource for people with mental disorders. The groups exist for a variety of conditions, including depression and bipolar disorder. Some are informal and are made up of only people with mental disorders. Others are clinic-sponsored and have professional moderators. Meetings are usually held in public spaces such as churches and community centers. Group members share tips for coping with problems, cheer each other's successes, and motivate each other to stay with treatment programs. Support groups are not substitutes for group therapy, psychotherapy, or prescribed medication.

Those wanting to join a support group should look for one that gives everyone a chance to share and will not be dominated by a few talkative people. Although most groups are reputable, some may be run by unscrupulous people. Groups that charge unreasonable fees or insist that members purchase products should be avoided.

Online support groups are also options, especially for people with limited mobility or transportation. However, meeting in person may be of greater psychological benefit because members can practice social skills and make friends. Those who choose online groups should be wary of disclosing personal information.

possibilities. The most crucial issue for them is to believe that they are worthy individuals and that getting better—and even complete recovery—is possible. Such positive thinking can offset the loss of self-esteem that can come as a result of a diagnosis.

PATIENT EMPOWERMENT

The sense of self-determination, the feeling of being in control of one's own life, is perhaps the most important factor for recovery. Self-determination is so basic to the worldview of healthy people that most people rarely think about it. They take for granted that they can live and work where they want and choose their own friends. People with mental disorders often lose these basic freedoms when they enter the mental health care system. Patients who feel adrift, as though they have no power over their destiny, can stall in their recovery process. The best outcomes occur when patients see themselves as active participants in their treatment and have the full expectation of a complete recovery. This kind of empowerment is a goal of modern psychiatric and psychological treatment.

The idea of patient empowerment is a positive one, but it has limits. For patients to participate

Caregivers can provide those with mental disorders the support they need to live in their communities.

in their own treatment, they need basic logic and decision-making capabilities. They need to be able to understand the various treatments so the benefits and risks of each can be weighed. At the minimum, such decisions require the patient to focus for some time and to think clearly.

The absence of those abilities is what prompted some patients to be placed in hospitals in the first place. This problem is addressed by treating patients under conditions of the greatest possible freedom on a case-by-case basis. Clients who are capable of making important decisions are given the opportunity to do so, while others work to regain that right. Less crucial decisions are left to the individual whenever possible.

EMPOWERMENT THROUGH SELF-ADVOCACY

Some people with mental disorders have trouble expressing their needs. Because they are poor communicators, they have not been listened to by others. This frustration may make them anxious and appear aggressive. But coaching can give them skills to be appropriately assertive and keep anxiety under control.

Communication skills are especially important after release from an institution. Routine errands, such as buying groceries, can become ordeals for some

Help for People Who Hear Voices

The Hearing Voices Network is a program that helps people with schizophrenia who have auditory hallucinations. The voices are usually upsetting, and medications do not always silence them. Psychologist Patricia Deegan said, "It seems that as a general rule, most mental health staff feel it is taboo to inquire into the voice hearing experience of the people they work with."[2] The network encourages patients with schizophrenia to talk about their voices and share coping strategies.

people with mental disorders if they do not obtain those skills. As a result, important tasks might go undone, which may lead to greater stress and anxiety. Community mental health workers sometimes assist recently released patients with particularly important responsibilities, such as obtaining medication.

COMMUNITY SUPPORT

Patients who have lived for extended periods of time in residential care settings often have trouble upon their release. Suicide rates are highest for depressed veterans immediately after their release. They require help and support to transition back into society.

Studies have shown that the quality of life of deinstitutionalized patients with mental disorders is highest when they have the means to satisfy their own needs, especially economically. Employment is a crucial step. Not only is self-esteem likely to be higher in people who can earn their own living, but the social contacts made at work help them feel accepted in their communities. It is a myth that people with mental disorders are capable of doing only simple work. They are often highly intelligent and capable of handling complex jobs, especially if their illnesses are managed with regular medication.

Some mental disorders, such as schizophrenia, begin in early adulthood when young adults are finishing college or establishing careers. This diminishes their earning power. Once symptoms are under control, schooling and careers can resume. Deinstitutionalized patients who finished school before their symptoms set in have the tools to begin professional careers. Other individuals may lack job skills and have no experience to fill a résumé. They can benefit from vocational programs that teach marketable skills.

RISKS OF SELF-DETERMINATION AND EMPOWERMENT

Self-determination means that patients may be in charge of important decisions when they are not thinking rationally. This entails some risk. One patient could decide

Employment Programs

Some vocational reha-bilitation programs for people with mental disor-ders are run as nonprofit businesses. They train people who have well-managed mental disorders to develop marketable skills. One such operation is an upholstery company in Massachusetts called Restoration Project, Inc. It is staffed entirely by out-patients. "Everything we do here is normal voca-tional training, skills built on top of skills, problem-solving. It is empowering if you want a person to go forward," says man-ager Eloise Newell.[3] Restoration Project, Inc., is set up with stations for each stage of production, so workers can decide where they want to work each day. The workers live independently and receive salaries.

to go off medication and have a mental breakdown. Another might choose to engage in risky or criminal behaviors that could injure himself or others.

Greater freedom for patients does mean that society takes a small degree of risk. Society counts on the judgment of professionals to decide which people can be treated in the community and which people will be best served in an institution.

Mistakes will be made because the system is a human one. Judges and juries decide whether criminals with mental disorders belong in prisons or in hospitals. Doctors decide how much freedom to give each patient without knowing exactly what each one might do. Each party within the mental health care system must help patients achieve all they can while balancing the rights of individuals and those of society.

Managed Care

Managed care is a controversial system intended to control costs of both physical and mental health care. Under managed care, inpatient admissions have been limited and lengths of hospital stays have been reduced. Depending on the plan, patients are allowed only a certain number of visits with psychotherapists. Managed care has been criticized for reducing the quality of care while trying to keep costs down.

*Mental health supporters work continuously to fight
the stigma of mental disorders.*

TIMELINE

2850 BCE	1402	1797
A medical facility opens in Egypt that humanely treats patients.	In England, St. Mary of Bethlehem hospital is converted into a mental asylum. It becomes known for its inhumane treatment of inmates.	William Hack Tuke opens a humane therapeutic mental health center in England.

1939–1945	1950s
Adolf Hitler's policies result in the deaths of 183,000 patients with mental disorders.	Successful new medications calm agitated or violent patients.

1874

The first U.S. law passes to prevent involuntary commitment to mental institutions.

1930s

Maine legislator Gail Laughlin sponsors a bill to penalize husbands who lie to commit their wives to mental institutions.

1968

The Fair Housing Act outlaws discrimination on the basis of race, religion, and disability.

1973

The American Psychiatric Association removes homosexuality from its list of mental illnesses.

TIMELINE

1975

O'Connor v. Donaldson prevents nonviolent patients with mental disorders from being involuntarily committed.

1990

The Americans with Disabilities Act prevents discrimination against people who are disabled.

2000

Global Burden of Disease reports mental disorders account for 12 percent of the burden of disease in developed countries.

2003

Sell v. United States allows forcible medication of defendants with a mental disorder to make them competent to stand trial.

1991

In a human rights resolution, the United Nations adopts the principles for the protection of people with mental disorders.

1996

The Mental Health Parity Act requires insurance companies with mental health services to make them equal to physical services.

2005

United States v. Booker allows judges to give defendants with mental disorders longer sentences than recommended by guidelines.

2006

Researchers find a gene that increases the risk of schizophrenia.

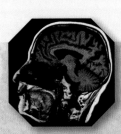

ESSENTIAL FACTS

AT ISSUE

❖ Throughout history, people with mental disorders have been treated inhumanely and discarded by society as crazy or possessed by evil spirits. While the stigma of mental disorders has lessened in recent decades, it is still prevalent.

❖ Approximately 26 percent of U.S. citizens ages 18 and older experience a mental disorder each year. Continued discussion and research of mental disorders is necessary for professionals to identify and treat them.

❖ A small percentage of people with mental disorders become violent. Medical professionals and other authorities work to protect both society and the individual with a mental disorder.

❖ In the twentieth century, several important pieces of legislation provided people with mental disorders equal civil rights in society.

CRITICAL DATES

1402
St. Mary of Bethlehem hospital was converted into a mental asylum in England. Bedlam, as it became known, treated patients with mental disorders inhumanely.

1975
The Supreme Court ruled in *O'Connor v. Donaldson* that nonviolent patients with mental disorders could not be involuntarily committed to mental hospitals.

1990
George H. W. Bush signed the Americans with Disabilities Act into law. The act prevents discrimination against people who are disabled in areas of employment, transportation, hotel accommodation, and other public services.

1996

The Mental Health Parity Act required insurance companies to make mental health services equal to physical health services.

Quotes

"Families say this is the only illness in the world where you don't get a covered dish. People don't call, don't inquire. The cultural understanding of mental illness is either that it's their fault for getting ill, or it's the fault of their family."—*Joyce Burland, national director of the Education, Training, and Peer Support Center at the National Alliance on Mental Illness, 2009*

"We are being misled by our own fears. We ought to be concerned about providing good treatment and helping people lead fulfilling lives, not obsessed with protecting ourselves from phantom threats that appear to be unrelated to mental illness."—*Paul Appelbaum, professor in Columbia University's Department of Psychiatry, 2009*

ADDITIONAL RESOURCES

SELECT BIBLIOGRAPHY

Carter, Rosalyn. *Helping Someone with Mental Illness*. New York: Three Rivers Press, 1999.

Darton, Katherine. "Notes on the History of Mental Health Care." *Mind.org*. 2009. 9 May 2009 <http://www.mind.org.uk/ Information/Factsheets/History+of+mental+health/Notes+on+the+ History+of+Mental+Health+Care.htm>.

Levy, Robert M., and Leonard S. Rubenstein. *The Rights of People with Mental Disabilities: An American Civil Liberties Union Handbook*. Carbondale, IL: Southern Illinois University Press, 1996.

Millon, Theodore. *Masters of the Mind*. Hoboken, NJ: John Wiley and Sons, 2004.

FOR FURTHER READING

Jamieson, Patrick E. *Mind Race: A Firsthand Account of One Teenager's Experience with Bipolar Disorder*. Oxford, England: Oxford University Press, 2006.

Szabo, Ross, and Melanie Hall. *Behind Happy Faces: Taking Charge of Your Mental Health*. Lanham, MD: National Book Network, 2007.

Williams, Mary E. *Mental Illness*. Farmington Hills, MI: Cengage Gale, 2006.

WEB LINKS

To learn more about mental disorders, visit ABDO Publishing Company online at **www.abdopublishing.com**. Web sites about mental disorders are featured on our Book Links page. These links are routinely monitored and updated to provide the most current information available.

FOR MORE INFORMATION

For more information on this subject, contact or visit the following organizations.

National Alliance on Mental Illness
2107 Wilson Boulevard, Suite 300, Arlington, VA 22201-3042
703-524-7600
www.nami.org
A leading advocacy organization for mental disorders, the National Alliance on Mental Illness focuses on three main areas—awareness, education, and advocacy—to inform the public and help those affected by mental disorders.

National Institute of Mental Health
6001 Executive Boulevard, Rockville, MD 20852
301-443-4513
www.nimh.nih.gov
The National Institute of Mental Health focuses on both the medical and social aspects of mental disorders. The organization's Web site provides information on the characteristics and treatment of specific mental disorders, as well as reports on new scientific advances.

GLOSSARY

amulet
A small object believed to have magical power to ward off harm if worn or carried.

anesthetize
To administer anesthesia in order to produce a loss of sensation.

auditory
Perceived through hearing.

bloodletting
The removal of blood in the attempt to cure an illness.

catatonic
Characterized by muscular rigidity and mental stupor, sometimes alternating with agitation.

commit
To legally place a person in a mental institution.

confine
To restrict movement or trap in a limited area.

criminality
Being a criminal or involved in illegal conduct.

debilitating
Causing a loss in health, strength, or energy.

defendant
A person or organization against whom charges are brought in a court of law.

deinstitutionalization
The release of psychiatric patients from an institution and into the community.

delusion
A false belief held despite evidence to the contrary, often as a result of a mental disorder.

discrimination
Unfavorable treatment of a person based on class, race, or group rather than individual merit.

electroshock therapy
> A treatment for mental disorders that puts electric currents in the brain to induce seizures.

euthanize
> To intentionally put to death, usually humanely and upon request.

evaluation
> A diagnostic study of a physical or mental condition.

genetic
> Having to do with genes, or the passing of biological characteristics from one generation to the next.

hallucination
> A perception of something imaginary through visual, auditory, olfactory, or tactile senses.

hereditary
> Genetic; inherited from parents and capable of being passed on to the next generation.

institutionalize
> To commit a person to an institution, often for psychiatric care.

invincibility
> Inability to lose in any contest or suffer harm or death.

paranoia
> The belief that others are always out to cause one harm.

paraplegia
> Paralysis of the legs due to spinal injury or disease.

psychotic
> A person who suffers from psychosis, which includes experiencing delusions and hallucinations.

psychotropic
> Affecting a person's mental state.

stigma
> A mark of disgrace associated with a certain characteristic.

Source Notes

Chapter 1. Individual and Societal Rights
1. Matt Lauer. "Interview with Tom Cruise." *MSNBC Online.* 25 Jun. 2005. 1 May 2009 <http://www.msnbc.msn.com/id/8343367/page/2/>.
2. Brooke Shields. "War of Words." *New York Times Online.* 1 Jul. 2005. 1 May 2009 <http://www.nytimes.com/2005/07/01/opinion/01shields.html>.
3. American Psychiatric Association. *Diagnostic and Statistical Manual of Mental Disorders.* 4th ed. Washington DC: American Psychiatric Association, 2000.
4. National Institute of Mental Health. "About NIMH." *NIMH Online.* 8 May 2009. 11 May 2009 <http://www.nimh.nih.gov/about/index.shtml>.

Chapter 2. A History of Mental Disorders
1. Harold G. Koenig. *Aging and God: Spiritual Pathways to Mental Health in Midlife and Later Years.* Binghamton, NY: Haworth, 1994. 12.

Chapter 3. Common Mental Disorders
1. David Carbonell. "First Steps to Recovery." *Anxietycoach.com.* 1 Jun. 2007. 11 May 2009 <http://www.anxietycoach.com/steps.htm>.
2. NAMI. "About NAMI." *NAMI.org.* 2009. 11 May 2009 <http://www.nami.org/Template.cfm?Section=About_NAMI&Template=/ContentManagement/ContentDisplay.cfm&ContentID=58580>.

Chapter 4. Overcoming Stigma

1. "Mental Illness Alone Is No Trigger for Violence." *USA Today Online*. 3 Feb. 2009. 11 May 2009 <http://www.usatoday.com/news/health/2009-02-03-mental-illness-violence_N.htm>.
2. Ibid.

Chapter 5. Impact of Mental Disorders
1. Vicki Koenig. "Mental Illness—Information for Families." *SPCSB. org*. Sanctuary House of Santa Barbara, Inc. 2006. 11 May 2009 <http://www.spcsb.org/articles/mental_illness.html>.

Chapter 6. Causes, Prevention, and Treatment
1. SZAdmin. "Studies Show How Stress Damages Young Brains." *Schizophrenia Daily News Blog*. 5 Mar. 2007. 11 May 2009 <http://www.schizophrenia.com/sznews/archives/004739.html>.

Chapter 7. Mental Disorders and the Law
1. Julie Wolf. "John Hinckley, Jr." *American Experience: Reagan: People and Events*. PBS/WGBH. 2000. 11 May 2009 <http://www.pbs.org/wgbh/amex/reagan/peopleevents/pande02.html>.
2. ACLU. "ACLU Requests Transfer of Mentally Ill Prisoners from Supermax." *American Civil Liberties Union Online*. 10 Aug. 2001. 11 May 2009 <http://www.aclu.org/disability/mentallydisabled/10632prs2 0010810.html>.
3. "Rosalynn Carter Addresses Pro Bono Luncheon." *ABAnet.org*. 12 Dec. 2006. 11 May 2009 <http://www.abanet.org/legalservices/probono/carter_speech.html>.

Source Notes Continued

Chapter 8. Patient Rights

1. "Judi Chamberlin Debates E. Fuller Torrey, MD on Involuntary Treatment: Should Forced Medication Be a Treatment Option in Patients with Schizophrenia?" *Power2U.org*. National Empowerment Center. 2008. 11 May 2009 <http://www.power2u.org/debate. html>.
2. Ibid.
3. Ibid.

Chapter 9. Recovery and Empowerment

1. Daniel Fisher. "Recovery from Schizophrenia: From Seclusion to Empowerment." *Medscape CME Web site*. 10 Mar. 2006. 11 May 2009 <http://www.medscape.com/viewarticle/523539_2>.
2. Patricia Deegan. "Hearing Voices that are Distressing: Self-Help Resources and Strategies." *Power2U.org*. National Empowerment Center. 2009. 11 May 2009 <http://www.power2u.org/articles/ selfhelp/voices.html>.
3. Richard Sherer. "Employment Programs Help Patients With Mental Illnesses Succeed." *Psychiatric Times* 20.13 (2003). 11 May 2009 <http://www.psychiatrictimes.com/display/ article/10168/47871>.

INDEX

Index Continued

ABOUT THE AUTHOR

Courtney Farrell is a full-time writer who has contributed to a dozen college-level biology textbooks and has authored several books for young people on social issues and historical events. She has a master's degree in zoology and is interested in conservation and sustainability issues. Farrell is certified as a designer and teacher of permaculture, a type of organic agriculture. She lives with her husband and sons on a ranch in the mountains of Colorado.

PHOTO CREDITS

Emrah Turudu/iStockphoto, cover, 13; Tammie Arroyo/AP Images, 6; Stuart Ramson/AP Images, 9; The Print Collector/ Photolibrary, 14; iStockphoto, 17, 96 (top); Barney Burstein/ Corbis, 25; Angel Herrero de Frutos/iStockphoto, 26, 96 (bottom); Dave Bowman/AP Images, 32; Eric Risberg/AP Images, 35; Macleod Pappidas/AP Images, 36, 97; Warren Ruda/AP Images, 40, 99 (top); Barry Thumma/AP Images, 45; Donald Stampfli/AP Images, 46, 98; Elliot Minor/AP Images, 48; Phil Coale/AP Images, 51; Chris Schmidt/iStockphoto, 55; Luis Carolos Torres/iStockphoto, 56, 99 (bottom); Brad Killer/ iStockphoto, 62; Steve Cole/iStockphoto, 65; Cheryl Guerrero/ AP Images, 66; Rogelio Solis/AP Images, 70; Gina Sanders/ Shutterstock Images, 75; David Sandell/AP Images, 76; Manuel Balce Cencta/AP Images, 79; Greg Gibson/AP Images, 85; Larry W. Smith/AP Images, 86; M. Spencer Green/AP Images, 90; Elise Amendola/AP Images, 95